# Potential!

**You've got it, but what are you doing about it?**

Eric Barker

Book produced in Great Britain 2014 by
Pixel Tweaks Publications, Ulverston, Cumbria.

Copyright © 2014 Eric Barker

The right of Eric Barker to be identified as the author of this work has been asserted by him in accordance with the Copyright, Designs and Patents Act 1988.

All rights reserved.
No part of this publication may be produced, stored in a retrieval system, or transmitted in any form or by any means (electronic, mechanical, photocopying, recording or otherwise) without the prior written permission of the author.

Any person who does any unauthorised act in relation to this publication may be liable to criminal prosecution and civil claims for damages.

Cover image © Can Stock Photo Inc. / iofoto

ISBN: 978-0-9927514-4-9

Graphic Design by Russell Holden
www.pixeltweakspublications.co.uk

Pixel tweaks
PUBLICATIONS
ULVERSTON · CUMBRIA

# Acknowledgements

I would like to thank the following people who have helped me in lots of ways to work on maximising my own potential and to finish this book.

My parents Eric and Marjorie Barker for showing me the way of faith and for nurturing in me a love for God and His word from a young age. You laid a good foundation.

Joanna Barker for saying "yes" and loving me despite my shortcomings

Bethany, Rosie and Lucy for being brilliant daughters. You are beautiful and precious.

Steve Rayment from New Day Ministries for asking the right question

Eric Dixon for being a "father in the Lord"

Pastor Fred Mckeown at Millom Community Church for all the positive encouragement and prayer.

Rev Alan Bing at Ulverston Parish Church for believing in me when I was experiencing defeat and giving me opportunities for ministry in spite of that.

Mrs. Sue Wiggins from Millom Baptist Church for being a great proofreader and corrector of errors.

*To the memory of my father,
Eric Cecil Barker (1934-1992)
He made his mark.*

# Contents

Chapter One
Maximising Potential ...............................10

Chapter Two
Maximising Resources:
What's that in your hand? .........................20

Chapter Three
Maximising Reality:
Where are we on the journey? ..................33

Chapter Four
Maximising Relationships:
Who are we with on the journey? .............42

Chapter Five
Four Barriers to maximising potential. ......51

Chapter Six
Five keys to get us over the barriers ..........60

Chapter Seven
Making every effort…. .............................71

Chapter Eight
Discovering life purpose and calling .........87

# Introduction
# How do we measure success?

I had just turned forty and felt that I had a reasonably comfortable life, enjoying running a small business, being a family man and as a committed follower of Jesus Christ. As part of my own personal development I attended a business seminar and found myself listening to a 24 year old salesman who looked like he had just left school. He was retelling the story of his rapid rise to success which was essentially about how he had made it big in double glazing, bought a red Ferrari and now works with top athletes as a motivational coach!

All well and good except that it appears that he is now trying to sell me his version of "successful living" as though it was a product, because he really believes that he has found "the secret"! Unfortunately I am unconvinced by the presentation which actually lacks real content and apart from a few quirky stories (which admittedly were well delivered) and a stunt with a karate chop to a piece of wood, by the end of the afternoon I am feeling frustrated and disappointed. However as I left the workshop feeling grumpy I could not shake the big questions now racing around my mind about the value and nature of true success.

Ultimately that underwhelming seminar launched

me on a personal quest to understand the meaning of success for me personally, which in turn has provoked some very positive changes in my own life and, as a result, within the lives of those with whom I have influence. It has made me more proactive and more intentional and better equipped to be an effective person in my circle of influence. In this book I have tried to articulate the results of this quest which essentially was an exercise in reconciling what I had discovered about success as seen by much of society and the ancient wisdom of Biblical principles as lived out by Jesus Christ of Nazareth, which seemed to clash considerably with the world view of much 21st century thinking, but were values which I had sought to live by for over 25 years.

For many, hearing the word **Success** immediately triggers images related to how much they earn, how big their house is and what kind of car they aspire to drive. Other people, on the other hand, would explain that for them success is about the quality of their relationships and how much they can maintain their own personal integrity on a day to day basis. For some, success might simply mean having the motivation to get out of bed in a morning, to face another day looking after a disabled family member, who requires constant attention and loving care. It seems that success is a relative concept, dependant on what measuring system we are using and upon the state of our own personal circumstances. And there lies the problem!

**The problem occurs whenever we are tempted to measure our achievements, experiences and contributions against somebody else's measuring stick or performance criteria and whenever we do that we often end up feeling like a dismal failure.**

For instance, I remember an incident shortly after the events described above, where I became very frustrated with myself, following a conversation with a friend, who was telling me enthusiastically about their own success story. Instead of sharing and celebrating their excitement I found myself feeling envious and wondering why I did not have a similar story of my own. Actually I did have plenty of stories to tell, it was just that his story at the time seemed grander and more worthy than any of mine. Sadly my little pity party meant that I missed a great learning opportunity to find out how my friend had actually achieved his success and also the pleasure of giving praise where praise was due.

However, the positive result was that it made me re-think and consolidate some lessons that I had learned over many years that eventually allowed me to put my frustrations, with the measuring and meaning of personal success, into a more resourceful perspective. I came away with three learning points.

1. God made me unique and no one else can do what I can do in the way that I do it or be the way that I can be in the way that I can be it and

so, as a result...

2. My success will look different to other people's success because my skills, abilities and priorities give me unique outcomes. (Assuming I am pro-actively using those gifts/skills)

3. Success rarely comes without first experiencing some failure...or in other words receiving feedback that our current actions may need to change if we desire a different outcome.

The conclusion of my reflection, reading and research about success was to try to summarize my thinking in a single statement, which after several attempts ended up looking like this...

**Success is intentionally making the effort, to maximise my own unique potential in each and every situation, regardless of whether the circumstances are helping me or hindering me.**

**However that left me with another question:**

**What does maximising my potential actually look like?**

Chapter One

# Maximising Potential

**Principle: we all have a potential that can be maximised.**

There is a great story recounted by a motivational speaker and trainer called Barbara Glanz who often speaks to the staff of various businesses of how they can make a positive difference at work. On one occasion she was speaking at a particular company where there was a young man called Jonny who worked in a grocery store helping customer's pack their bags at the checkout. Johnny the bagger, as he has become known, had Down's syndrome. As a result of what he heard that day Johnny decided that even as a mere bagger he could make a difference and he began to take action in order to do so. Every night after work he would sit down and think of something positive, some reminder of how precious life is, how special people are, or of how many gifts we are surrounded by. Helped by his father, he would type this "thought of the day" on a strip of paper and make 300 copies of it, and Johnny would then sign each one.

The next day while bagging customer's groceries, Johnny would place one of his "thoughts for the day" in the top of the bags and say, "I've put a great saying in your bag. I hope it helps you have a good day. Thanks for coming."

Several months later, the store manager was astounded by what was happening in his store. Johnny's checkout line was always three times longer than anyone else's and during very busy periods when it was announced that other checkout lines were open, no one would move. Shoppers would say, "That's okay. I'll wait. I really want to get Johnny's thought for the day."

Before long Johnny's actions had transformed the entire store as his example began to positively impact other employees in the store. The floral department which used to throw away unused or broken corsages began to go out into the aisles, find an elderly woman or little girl and pin it on her. The butchers started putting ribbons on the cuts of meat which they were wrapping up for customers. Soon everyone in the store was inspired by Johnny's creative idea, and the customers for their part responded with enthusiastic loyalty which resulted in record sales over a long period of time.

Johnny was doing something that he could do; he was adding value to his own contribution in the workplace and more importantly to the lives and daily experiences of the hundreds of people that he served so well each day. He did this despite having a serious disability, a mundane and low paid job, without any obvious power or influence and using only the resources that were immediately available to him. He simply made the most of who he was and what he had. He was maximising his potential. If you type "Jonny the bagger" into Google you will find that this story has gone viral and is now impacting people all over the world every single day.

Viktor Frankl wrote Man's Search for Meaning, a book which has riveted generations of readers with its descriptions of life in Nazi death camps and its lessons for spiritual survival. Between 1942 and 1945 Frankl, a psychiatrist, suffered in four different camps, including Auschwitz, while his parents, brother, and pregnant wife perished. Based on his own experience and the stories of his many patients, Frankl argues in the book that we cannot avoid suffering but we can choose how to cope with it, find meaning in it, and move forward with renewed purpose.

"What man actually needs," Frankl writes, "is not a tensionless state but rather the striving and struggling for a worthwhile goal, a freely chosen task . . . the call of a potential meaning waiting to be fulfiled by him."

In the years since its first publication in 1959, *Man's Search for Meaning* has become a classic, with more than twelve million copies in print around the world. In 1991 a Library of Congress survey asking readers to name a "book that made a difference in our life" found Man's Search for Meaning to be amongst the ten most influential books in America. Frankl, rather than becoming bitter and resentful as a result of his suffering, instead became a powerful influence for good in the lives of the thousands who have heard his story and read his books.

**Frankl refused to allow his extreme suffering to have the final word. He was maximising his potential.**

Of course history is littered with stories of ordinary people who maximised their potential often in the midst of circumstances that were stacked against them and their triumph over adversity serves as a reminder and an inspiration to us that we too can choose to be maximisers within our own circle of influence right here and right now. It is also true to say that we don't have to necessarily be facing difficulty in order to maximise potential, we can and should make it our business to be the best we can be through the good times when things are going well and life is sweet. I mean why wouldn't we?

## Becoming a Maximiser!

The idea of maximising our potential from a purely humanistic perspective is about being able to do absolutely anything that we want to do just because we put our mind to it and take massive action to make it happen. There is of course much to be said in favour of this kind of thinking and it's a no brainer to see that any kind of effort and focus will undoubtedly produce better results than no effort and little focus.

However the Biblical world-view has a different and an actually more empowering emphasis that goes way beyond the achieving of goals and tasks. In this paradigm humans are not random accidents of nature, we are not related to apes, and we are not an evolved bunch of cells that have accidentally learned to walk, talk, think and make creative choices. Far from it, there is a design and there is a designer!

The implications of this paradigm reveal that we are created with a unique design, bearing the image of God and intended for a specific purpose. Moreover within that context we each have a personal calling or destiny to fulfil. I personally find this so much easier to believe than any theory which asks us to accept that we are the result of a random series of chemical reactions and improbable coincidences which to my simple mind requires a huge leap of faith to even consider that as being a possibility. Especially as science itself has proven the intricate design features of the Universe that allow it to work with perfect precision and within a series of natural laws that strongly suggest both a designer and a lawgiver behind it all.

The concept that we are made in God's image is difficult to understand because we immediately reach out for visual clues when the truth is so much more than skin deep.

Our reflection of God's image includes:

- Intellect. The ability to think, abstractly, i.e., put words to ideas, think in cause-effect relationships, remember. Man also has the ability to know the difference between right and wrong.
- Emotions. The ability to feel passion, patience, joy, and so much more.
- Will. The ability to make judgments, decisions, i.e., choices based on intellect and emotions.
- Self perception. The ability to know one's self i.e., self consciousness and self awareness.
- Self direction. The ability to plan, dream or envision a future state.

**The implications of believing that we were intentionally designed by a thinking, feeling, choosing and communicating creator leads to the conclusion that …maximising our potential is literally becoming everything that we were made to be.**

The progressive and ongoing discovery of this life purpose is surely an invitation to the most thrilling adventure ride ever imagined. Just being aware of the hand of the creator, designer and architect of the universe brings into focus the idea that successful living is not simply about the achievement of great deeds and great results for their own sake. The implication is that we are all people of destiny and purpose in the context of a much bigger cosmic plan. Implicit in this idea is the reality that we can only fulfil our potential in partnership with the One who conceived the plan in the first place. In other words the first step on the ever unfolding journey towards truly maximising our potential is to get to know the one who made us!

## Losing our lives in order to find them?

However there is a strange paradox that needs to be understood before we can fully embrace all that God wants us to possess. In trying to communicate the ways of God to us Jesus Christ taught that in order to find our life (i.e. our true self) we had first of all to lose it (i.e. our false self)! In other words before we can maximise our life, we first of all have to give it up by choice! One preacher summed it up in an easy to remember phrase that has been often repeated as "letting go and letting God". Living life to the max then apparently starts by surrendering our lives in the knowledge and service of God and giving up our rights rather than spending our lives defending them. The measure of success is not about how much we get but about how much we can give and our status in this new kind of kingdom is not based on how powerful we are but on the quality of our servant hearts and our relationship with the King.

Jim Elliot a missionary who was martyred for his faith in the 1950's was probably thinking along these lines when he famously penned the words

> **"He is no fool who gives what he cannot keep to gain what he cannot lose"**

So it turns out that in accepting the invitation of Jesus to follow Him, maximising our potential is actually about the significance that comes through sacrifice and service, it is about the greatness that comes through giving ourselves away, it is about the wholeness that comes as we are totally spoiled for the ordinary as our hearts are forever transformed by the power and love of a God who reveals himself as our heavenly father.

We learn to maximise our potential as we work in partnership with Him, so that we do what we can do and He does what we cannot do. We do the possible and leave the impossible to the one for whom nothing is too difficult. We become co-workers with Him, partners in a cosmic creative plan that is bigger than our minds can fathom and yet the reality of it resonates in our hearts in ways that words cannot express. The scriptures describe how this process works in Ephesians 3:20 which states that God "is able to do immeasurably more than all we ask or imagine, according to his power *that is at work within us*". This is an awesome concept that requires some serious consideration that the God of the universe actually flows through us and works with us, not in spite of us.

However just knowing that we are in this partnership with God does not mean that our success is guaranteed, there is still much for us to do, decisions only we can make, choices only we can take and actions only we can carry out. This reality requires a response of proactive faith which is the opposite of a very common attitude which could be described as a "whatever will be, will be" passive state of mind.

In the context of "proactive faith" Maximising our Potential means, doing what we can do that we've not yet done, becoming what we could be that we've not yet become and accomplishing things that we could achieve that we've not even tried out yet. It means overcoming the fear of the future, embracing challenge and change, ditching disappointment and cultivating hope and when the going gets tough being the one who keeps on keeping on.

So, if we believe that we were actually "made for something" and, more importantly, someone greater than ourselves, and that the meaning of life and success is not to acquire stuff, or power, or fame and fortune but to contribute/serve using our unique skill set and gifting, as we work in partnership with God rather than for Him, then more specifically maximising our potential is about:

- Adding value with our unique contribution,
- Improving the quality of our contribution
- Increasing options and enhancing our life choices for ourselves and others
- Enlarging the vision of what is possible regardless of our circumstances
- Helping others to grow and develop their own unique potential.
- Finding significance through service and sacrifice.

There are three areas that are common to all where we can intentionally become maximisers by adding value, improving, enhancing and developing our unique and individual life contribution in order to make a significant difference for the better.

1. **Resources: what we have available to us right now.**

2. **Reality: where we are in our life journey right now**

3. **Relationships: who we have influence and interaction with on a daily basis.**

Over the next few chapters we will unpack these areas in a little more detail to see how we can make personal and practical improvements to our individual lives in these vital segments of our experience.

Chapter Two

# Maximising Resources: What's that in your hand?

**Principle: We maximise our resources when they are made available to God**

In the well known Old Testament story of Moses recounted in the book of Exodus we meet the young Jewish boy who, having been rescued from certain death and brought up as a prince by an Egyptian princess, ends up many years later, living in the desert looking after his father-in-law's sheep. He has arrived in the desert after running away from the palace of Pharaoh following an incident where he kills a slave driver who is maltreating one of his fellow Israelites. So here he is, many years later, living in obscurity tending sheep and not making any plans to do anything extraordinary any time soon. His upbringing as a prince and the privilege and comfort that was part of his growing up now seems a distant and almost irrelevant memory and any dreams of being or doing something of significance are well and truly buried.

However suddenly and dramatically God appears to him and tells him that he is going to be the one to rescue the Jews from slavery in Egypt and that he, Moses, is to go and speak personally to Pharaoh and demand the release of the Jews. Naturally Moses is skeptical and despite the incredible nature of the manifest presence of God in a burning bush, complete with audible voice, he still manages to come up with lots of reasons as to why this is not such a good idea. Most of his reasons are to do with his own lack of natural ability and low self esteem which is revealed through his continual self deprecation and a singular focus on his own weaknesses. However in the midst of all this prevarication God patiently asks him a direct question.

"Moses, what is that in your hand"?

Now Moses did not have anything special in his hands , he actually had a shepherds staff or rod which was really just a piece of wood used in his work with sheep and maybe serving as something to lean on when he got tired. Just a piece of wood of no particular value and used in a very basic type of work, BUT when God had got through with Moses that ordinary wooden staff became a sign and a symbol of power and deliverance for the next 40 years. If we take the time to read the account in the book of Exodus we will see that as Moses leads the people of Israel through the desert to the Promised Land, the rod is used time and time again to demonstrate and initiate the miraculous power of God, at the dividing of the Red Sea, when water poured from a rock in the desert, to convince Pharaoh of Moses authority and so on.

Maybe we, like Moses, think that we don't have much to offer and we cannot really believe that what we have in our hands will ever amount to much in terms of success and productivity, but when we are willing to let God have what we have in our hands then He can do something amazing through us too. In fact whenever we give something back to God he always does something amazing with it. He always increases its value and effectiveness and produces much fruit in our lives from our acts of surrender and sacrifice.

For instance, remember the feeding of the five thousand which is recounted in the gospel accounts in the New Testament. We read that Jesus feeds five thousand plus people with just three loaves and two fishes, which had originally been intended as the packed lunch of a small boy, who was just an insignificant part of the large gathering following Jesus that day. We quickly see, however, that when God is invited into the picture, nothing remains small and insignificant. Jesus takes a packed lunch for one and provides a magnificent feast for five thousand. Something mundane becomes the vehicle for the miraculous. The insignificant takes on a divine magnificence that goes way beyond expectations. A huge catering problem becomes a platform for a demonstration of Gods power and provision, revealing at the same time a glimpse of the compassionate, generous heart of our Heavenly Father.

So what is in your hands? What skills qualities or talents and or resources do you have that might seem small and insignificant but that in partnership with the divine nature can be transformed into something with impact and significance?

While we are thinking about that lets look at two significant areas in which we can maximise our resources in partnership with God: our talents and our time.

## 1. Maximising Our Talents

Principle: Each person has been given a set of unique talents which require development in order to be fruitful and effective.

Everybody has a set of natural skills and abilities which often go undiscovered or are under used because of a lack of awareness, the fear of failure and a general lack of self esteem. Even for those of us who realise what we possess, we still underestimate what can be done with it and instead of confidently celebrating and investing in it we mistakenly obscure our talent in a veil of excuses, false pride and unfavourable comparisons with others whose talents we perceive as superior to our own. This is not a new phenomenon and in fact Jesus recognized the problem when he told the story of the three servants and their investments in Matthew. Take time to read that passage now and reflect on what lessons there are here for you.

## Matthew 25:14-27 (The Message)
## The Story about Investment

*₁₄₋₁₈"It's also like a man going off on an extended trip. He called his servants together and delegated responsibilities. To one he gave five thousand dollars, to another two thousand, to a third one thousand, depending on their abilities. Then he left. Right off, the first servant went to work and doubled his master's investment. The second did the same. But the man with the single thousand dug a hole and carefully buried his master's money.*

*₁₉₋₂₁"After a long absence, the master of those three servants came back and settled up with them. The one given five thousand dollars showed him how he had doubled his investment. His master commended him: 'Good work! You did your job well. From now on be my partner.'*

*₂₂₋₂₃"The servant with the two thousand showed how he also had doubled his master's investment. His master commended him: 'Good work! You did your job well. From now on be my partner.'*

*₂₄₋₂₅"The servant given one thousand said, 'Master, I know you have high standards and hate careless ways, that you demand the best and make no allowances for error. I was afraid I might disappoint you, so I found a good hiding place and secured your money. Here it is, safe and sound down to the last cent.'*

*26-27"The master was furious. 'That's a terrible way to live! It's criminal to live cautiously like that! If you knew I was after the best, why did you do less than the least? The least you could have done would have been to invest the sum with the bankers, where at least I would have gotten a little interest.*

**THINK: How are you investing your talents today?**

**Are you burying a talent because you are afraid of people's reactions and opinions?**

**Unearth your talent bury your fear!**

Remember when it comes to talents **we are not average, we are unique** therefore there is something that we can do in a specific way that no one else can do and the world is a poorer place when we fail to make the most of what God has given. We have the responsibility to take what we have and to invest it so that whatever it is will increase and develop ensuring a healthy return on our investment and an effective use of our time and talents. Jesus himself said that it was God the Father's express desire that we bear "much fruit" to His glory.

So in order to maximise our potential we must make the effort to discover what we have in our hands in terms of gifts and abilities, then celebrate them, invest in them, practice them, and finally use them to contribute and create something beautiful, as we prayerfully present them back to God.

The deal is we must pro-actively and intentionally do what we can do with what we have been given and trust God to do what we cannot do! We do the possible and God will do the impossible!

- What have you got in you that you can bring to Jesus so that he can multiply and maximise it?
- Are you playing safe with your talent or going out on a limb to risk making the most of it?
- Are you fully aware of what and who you are in relation to your skills qualities and values?

## Practical reflective exercises

Here are a couple of simple exercises to help identify your strengths and skills so that you can focus on them and develop them intentionally in the future.

*Exercise one:* A personal SWOT analysis:

Use this exercise to help focus on your strengths and reflect on how you can use them to make the most of opportunities in your life and to overcome threats. Be honest and be bold and don't underestimate the powerful effect that happens when we focus on our strengths instead of trying to improve our weaknesses. It's important to be aware of your weaknesses, but much more effective and productive to use your energy developing or maximising your strengths.

***Exercise two:*** Skills, Qualities and Values grid. Start by thinking of yourself in three specific areas.

- Our skills and abilities: these are either a natural talent or a learned ability that can be developed.

- Our qualities and characteristics: these are a result of our life choices and personality preferences.

- Our values and beliefs: these represent how we see the world and what our priorities are in life.

In order to help identify what these are complete the questions in the grid and review your answers picking up on themes and links across the grid to form an overview of what you can do, who you are and what you value.

Then ask yourself...

- Where am I using these skills right now and am I using them to their full potential?

- Are the characteristics and qualities that I have identified helping me or hindering me?

- Are my values helpful or hurtful to my cause?

- What needs to change in me to take me forward in my life journey?

- What is God saying to me about using my personal strengths?

# Personal SWOT ANALYSIS: list your strengths, weaknesses, opportunities and threats before answering the questions.

| Translate into tasks for action planning | Strengths you know you have. | Weaknesses you are aware of. |
|---|---|---|
| Opportunities that are open to you now | How do I use these strengths to take advantage of these opportunities? | How do I overcome the weaknesses that prevent me taking advantage of these opportunities? |
| Threats you face right now | How do I use these strengths to reduce the likelihood and impact of these threats? | How do I address the weaknesses that will make these threats a reality? |

| Qualities to develop | Skills to gain/improve/develop | Values and beliefs to hold onto. |
|---|---|---|
| Think of someone who inspires you. What qualities in them do you admire and wish to copy? | List 3 things you really enjoy doing now and 3 skills you would love to be able to do in the future | Imagine a steel beam 6 inches wide strung across 2 skyscrapers. What would it take for you to be willing to walk across that beam? |
| Are you displaying any of the qualities at the moment? Are you willing to change your behaviour in order to be more like that person? | What do you want to achieve by learning these new skills? | What is it about this thing that makes you so passionate and courageous? |
| 10 years from today a local newspaper runs a story about your life and success. What are they saying about you? | If you could spend a full day learning from a world class expert in any subject or skill of your choosing what skill or subject expertise would you really want to discover. | If you could spend 1 hour with anybody from any period of history. Who would it be and why? |
| What do you need to start doing now for this to be true in 10 years time? What is the first step towards this long term goal? | What do you want to gain from this opportunity? | What would you hope to gain from this one hour? |

## 2. Maximising our Resources : Time

**Principle: We all have the same amount of time and so it is not about the amount of time that we have but about what we do within the framework of those hours, days, weeks and years that makes us more or less effective.**

- What are you doing with your time?
- Are you spending time or investing it?
- Are you planning your life or simply drifting along taking things as they come.
- Are you being intentional about your life or is it a case of whatever will be will be?

For many years as a teenager and into my early twenties I had no desire to plan my time preferring instead to be spontaneous (and I believed inspired) which I was very good at and I did manage in many circumstances to fly by the seat of my pants and still make things work, despite a lack of planning and preparation. However, I eventually began to realise that often I could have done so much better and worked more easily with others if I had invested some time planning my days and weeks and preparing for events and tasks with some forethought. I began to make some changes and started to use a time planner and as time went on the changes began to stick. Admittedly it has not been something that has come naturally to me but over the years as I have become increasingly more thoughtful and intentional about my schedule I have noticed the following benefits.

1. I am able to fit more things into my life because I now have a plan and a set of priorities

2. I am able to achieve a better outcome from things that I have prepared for because I have made the time to prepare for them.

3. I enjoy the anticipation of looking forward to events that I have planned for in advance.

4. I work better with other people because they know what I am doing in advance and can schedule their own lives and priorities so we can work more closely and effectively as a team.

5. I have got better at saying "NO!" to things as I now have a set of principles that help me set my own agenda instead of being driven by other people's agendas.

## Practical Application

Keep an hourly log of how you use your time over the period of a week and then ask yourself the following questions.

- Am I in control of my schedule or is it in control of me?

- Am I being proactive or reactive in my use of time?

- What should I be saying "NO" to in order to release time for more important things?

- What's missing from my life that I really need to introduce and make time for?

- Is the use of my time congruent with my beliefs and values?

- If I gave God charge of my schedule for the week how would it read?

Chapter Three

# Maximising Reality: Where are we on the journey?

> Principle: It's not what happens to us but what happens <u>in us</u> that makes the difference and dictates the long term outcomes in our lives.

- Are you in a place of opposition or a place of opportunity?
- Are you facing problems or possibilities?
- Are you adapting to your circumstances or are you controlled by them?
- Are you responding to your current reality with fear or faith?

We need to understand that how we respond to what's happening to us determines the results of what will happen in us and therefore the kind of person we end up becoming. We can decide now before they happen, how we are going to respond to the challenges and changes that life brings to us and intentionally plan and determine to overcome fear with faith, see problems as possibilities and embrace opposition as an opportunity.

Once again the Bible has a prime example of the principle at work in the account of Joseph in Genesis 36-42 which is briefly summarized below.

## Joseph the dreamer...
## everything's groovy...well almost!

Joseph, son of Jacob and Rachel, lived in the land of Canaan with ten half-brothers, one full brother and one half-sister. He was Rachel's firstborn and Israel's eleventh son. Of all the sons, Joseph was loved by his father the most. Jacob even arrayed Joseph with a coat of many colours and his father's obvious favouritism caused his half brothers to hate him. When Joseph was seventeen years old he had two dreams that he believed were from God. In the first dream, Joseph and his brothers gathered bundles of grain. Then, all of the grain bundles that had been prepared by the brothers gathered around Joseph's bundle and bowed down to it. In the second dream, the sun (father), the moon (mother) and eleven stars (brothers) bowed down to Joseph himself. When he naively shared these two dreams with his brothers, they despised him all the more for what they saw as pride and arrogance and the implication that the family would be bowing down to Joseph. They began to plot his demise.

## Joseph in a pit...
## things get difficult...

While they were feeding the flocks a long way from home, the brothers saw Joseph coming to visit them and plotted to kill him. However, the eldest brother, Reuben suggested that they have Joseph thrown into an empty cistern until they could figure out what to do with him. He intended to rescue Joseph and return him to his father. Unaware of their intent, Joseph approached his brothers, they turned on him and stripped him of the coat his father had made for him, and threw him into the cistern. As they pondered what to do with Joseph, the brothers see a camel caravan of Ishmaelite's carrying spices and perfumes to Egypt for trade, and sell Joseph into slavery for twenty pieces of silver.

## Joseph in slavery...
## they get even more difficult...

Joseph is sold to serve Potiphar, the captain of Pharaoh's guard. While serving in Potiphar's household, the Bible asserts that God was with Joseph so that he prospered in everything he did and found favour in the sight of Potiphar and became his personal servant. Eventually Joseph was promoted to oversee Potiphar's entire household as a superintendent. After some time, Potiphar's wife began to desire Joseph and sought to have an affair with him. Despite her persistence, he refused to have sex with her for fear of sinning against God. After some days of begging for him, she grabbed him by his cloak, but he escapes from her leaving his garment behind. Angered by his rejection she makes a false claim against him by accusing him of attempted rape. This results in Joseph being thrown into prison

**Joseph in prison...
how bad can it possibly get?**

Even in prison Joseph continues to find favour and the warden puts him in charge of the other prisoners. Soon afterward Pharaoh's chief cup bearer and chief baker, who had offended the Pharaoh, were thrown into the prison and they both have dreams, which Joseph interprets. The chief cup bearer had held a vine in his hand, with three branches that brought forth grapes; he took them to Pharaoh and put them in his cup. The chief baker had three baskets of bread on his head, intended for Pharaoh, but some birds came along and ate the bread. Joseph told them that within three days the chief cup bearer would be reinstated but the chief baker would be hanged. Joseph requested the cup bearer to mention him to Pharaoh and secure his release from prison, but the cup bearer, reinstalled in office, forgets Joseph who remains in prison for two more years. After this disappointing interlude Pharaoh has two dreams which disturb him. He dreams of seven lean cows which rise out of the river and devour seven fat cows; and, of seven withered ears of grain which devour seven fat ears. Pharaoh's wise men are unable to interpret these dreams, but the chief cup bearer remembers Joseph and speaks of his skill to Pharaoh. Joseph is called for, and interprets the dreams as foretelling that seven years of abundance would be followed by seven years of famine, and advises Pharaoh to store surplus grain during the years of abundance.

## Joseph Prince of Egypt...
## Dreams can come true!

Pharaoh acknowledges that Joseph's proposal to store grain during the abundant period is very wise and therefore releases him from prison and puts him in charge over "all the land of Egypt". Pharaoh even takes off his signet ring and put it on Joseph's hand, clothing him in fine linen and putting a gold necklace around his neck. During the following seven years of abundance, Joseph ensured that the storehouses were full and that all produce was measured until there was so much that it became immeasurable. When the famine did come, it was so severe that people from surrounding nations came to Egypt to buy bread as this nation was the only Kingdom prepared for the seven year drought. Eventually Joseph's family also come to buy grain and in the process of doing so bow down before him so fulfiling the dreams given many years before.

The story ends with forgiveness and reconciliation between Joseph and his brothers and the whole family settles in Egypt.

## Application:

Joseph was clearly a man of destiny, a dreamer, and a visionary. However before he could live out his dreams and achieve his potential there was much he had to endure in order to reach the place where he was fully equipped and mature enough to implement the actions required for those dreams to become real. Before he was promoted to the palace he had to suffer the hatred of his family, betrayal, slavery, false accusation, imprisonment and finally being forgotten by people whom he had helped. Yet despite all this he still continues to find favour in the eyes of God and man and in the midst of the direst circumstances stands out as a man of integrity and reliable character.

Essentially Joseph was on a journey of maturity where his goals and dreams were tested along with his character. The testing does its work, Joseph responds positively and at the end of the story he is able to acknowledge that even the bad things that others had intended for evil God has intended for good.

Most of us will probably never experience the depth of suffering that Joseph endured to reach his destiny but we will find opposition and problems blocking our way on many occasions. The test is will we give up and remain in the pit of despair or will we continue to trust God, and make every effort to press on to the promise?

**So if we are to maximise our potential in the midst of our own Reality we would be wise to emulate Joseph's three fold strategy of perseverance, faithfulness and purity.**

**Perseverance:** Choosing to be intentional about keeping on keeping on when the going gets tough and our dreams and desires seem to be thwarted by circumstances beyond our control. One of the Proverbs written by King Solomon resonates with this kind of long term approach to life and life planning by observing that "the end is better than the beginning and patience is better than pride".

Jesus himself says in Luke 9:62 *"No one who puts a hand to the plough and looks back is fit for service in the kingdom of God."*

The Apostle Paul said in Philippians 3:12-14: *"Not that I have already obtained all this, or have already arrived at my goal, but I press on to take hold of that for which Christ Jesus took hold of me. Brothers and sisters, I do not consider myself yet to have taken hold of it. But one thing I do: Forgetting what is behind and straining toward what is ahead, I press on toward the goal to win the prize for which God has called me heavenward in Christ Jesus."*

Other philosophers and thinkers have made similar observations over the centuries about the value of perseverance:

*"There is no failure except in no longer trying."* Elbert Hubbard

*"Great works are performed, not by strength, but by perseverance."* Dr. Samuel Johnson

*"In the confrontation between the stream and the rock, the stream always wins – not through strength but by perseverance."* H. Jackson Brown

**Faithfulness:** Choosing to honour God and believe that God is at work in our circumstances for our long term good and that His promises are reliable and His principles promote success. In other words no matter what is happening to us our decision to trust God and do the right thing is crucial to our long term success. This requires a long term view and an attitude of enduring hope which is fuelled by a positive imagination of the future which is captured in the words of King David in Psalms 27 when he says

"What would have become of me unless I had believed that I would see the goodness of the Lord in the land of the living?"

**Purity:** Choosing to maintain our integrity in the midst of temptation to compromise:

Compromising on the fundamentals is never a good option even though it might seem an easy option at the time.

Gandhi wisely observed that *"All compromise is based on give and take, but there can be no give and take on fundamentals. Any compromise on mere fundamentals is surrender. For it is all give and no take."*

Like Joseph we will discover that sometimes in order to maintain our integrity we have no other option than to flee from the temptation that confronts us. The choice to do that may have some negative consequences on some occasions but at least in the bigger scheme of things we will be able to look back in the longer term and know we did the right thing. The alternative is to live under a cloud of guilt shame and regret which, left to fester can destroy our ability to function and reduce our potential to be a maximiser

## Reflective Questions

What one thing do you know you need to keep doing in order to succeed?

Do you value faithfulness and loyalty above fame and celebrity?

What long term negative consequences can you identify in your current circumstances because you know you compromised your integrity in the past? How will you overcome those consequences and move towards future success?

Chapter Four

# Maximising Relationships: Who are we with on the journey?

### Principle: We are made for relationship

Since our entire lives are lived out in the context of relationships, it is vital that we become successful in all of our interactions with others. If we don't intentionally nurture our relationships they can easily become distant or strained. It is also true that whilst relationships can be the most rewarding and enhancing features of life, they can at times also be very difficult and even painful and we all know from experience that the people we love the most are the ones who have the power to hurt us the most. The converse is of course very true, that it is the people who love us the most who are most often hurt deeply when our own actions and words are unthinking and selfish.

- How then can we survive the potential for being rejected and let down when we make ourselves vulnerable in relationships?

- How can we also reduce the impact of our own unthinking and selfish tendencies?

- How can we make the most of our relationships

and be someone who contributes and energizes other people in our circles of influence rather than being a drain?

- The Bible has plenty of things to say about conducting positive healthy relationships and the following four keys are an attempt to distill the main themes.

## 1. The Habit of Forgiveness: Letting people go free.

We might as well face it no matter how good our relationships are sooner or later we are going to get hurt. A wrong word, a bitter criticism, a disagreement, rejection, disappointment are all factors that eventually show up even in the closest relationships. That being the case we need to develop the habit of forgiveness so that we can quickly let go of our hurt, let go of our desire for revenge and move on to reconcile and live in harmony again with the one who has hurt us.

When we know and have experienced how much God loves and forgives us it helps motivate us to develop a habit of letting go of resentment and hurt quickly so that we can achieve reconciliation and maintain friendships in the long term.

In addition to our proper response to what we have received there is also a host of medical research that indicates very strongly that clinging to betrayals, hurts and disappointments is bad for the body and mind.

Clinical psychologist Ryan Howes, who is based in Pasadena, California recently stated in a news article published on the web in 2011 that...

"It's inevitable that we'll all be hurt by others, and that it will happen often. People have accidents, make mistakes, behave selfishly, and even intentionally try to hurt one another. We can't escape it. Forgiveness is a vulnerable act that can feel like it opens us up to more pain. But we need to have a way to process and let go of the effects of injury, or we risk serious physical and emotional consequences."

Experts across the medical profession have concluded that forgiving those who have wronged us helps lower blood pressure, cholesterol, and heart rate plus is associated with a reduction in levels of depression, anxiety, and anger. One study found that forgiveness is associated with improved sleep quality, which has a strong effect on health. And in Duke University USA researchers reported a strong correlation between forgiveness and strengthened immunity among HIV-positive patients.

It seems then that people who forgive tend to have better relationships, feel happier and more optimistic, and overall enjoy better psychological well-being. Conversely holding onto our grudges and desiring some kind of retribution will only do damage to our well-being not to the person we are determined to hate.

Jesus talked a lot about forgiveness as did the writers of the letters to new churches. Here is a selection that summarises the approach that ultimately provides the basis for strong positive relationships.

*"And when you stand praying, if you hold anything against anyone, forgive them, so that your Father in heaven may forgive you your sins." Mark 11:25*

*"Do not judge, and you will not be judged. Do not condemn, and you will not be condemned. Forgive, and you will be forgiven." Luke 6:37*

*"Be kind and compassionate to one another, forgiving each other, just as in Christ God forgave you." Ephesians 4:32*

*"Bear with each other and forgive one another if any of you has a grievance against someone. Forgive as the Lord forgave you." Colossians 3:13*

## 2. The habit of Mercy: Giving people the benefit of the doubt or not giving people the judgment that we think they deserve.

*Blessed are the merciful, for they will be shown mercy. Matthew 5:7*

*For in the same way you judge others, you will be judged, and with the measure you use, it will be measured to you. Matthew 7:2*

Mercy is a broad term that refers to benevolence, forgiveness and kindness in a variety of ethical, religious, social and legal contexts. Loving mercy is one of three top priorities the prophet Micah in the Old Testament was encouraged to practice when he pondered about Gods general requirements for mankind. God responded with this statement:

*"He has shown you, Oh man, what is good and what the Lord requires, to do justly, <u>to love mercy</u> and to walk humbly with your God." Micah 6:8*

Essentially, mercy is about withholding judgment even when the person deserves it, and that is a beautiful thing to see in action. The ability to allow people to escape judgment when they deserve it is, in the final analysis, God's domain, but he allows us a glimpse of the power and triumph of mercy in our day to day lives. Mercy literally triumphs over judgment when we get the chance to withhold anger from those who deserve it, to withhold retribution and revenge when humanly speaking it is justified, to be generous to those who themselves are miserly, to be loving to those whose first instinct is to hate, to speak kindly to those who would never lift a finger to help us.

The pay back of giving mercy is that those who give mercy will also receive it and there will always be a time when we need it. So that's a good reason in itself to make it a part of our relationship building approach.

To quote Portia in Shakespeare's Merchant of Venice:

*"The quality of mercy is not strain'd.
It droppeth as the gentle rain from heaven
upon the place beneath. It is twice blest:
It blesseth him that gives and him that takes..."*

## 3. The habit of Modelling: treating other people in the same way that we ourselves would like to be treated.

What we give is what we get or to put it another way what we sow we will also reap. This is a universal and timeless principle and yet we often forget the implications of this truth. No one is exempt from it and we will all face the consequences of foolish actions and words should we choose to sow them and that is just the way it is. So treating others in the same way as we want to be treated is actually a very rewarding habit to cultivate, we get a great payback and our circle of friendship grows. The Golden rule as it has become known is found in the teachings of many religions and philosophies but it is most positively expressed by Jesus when he says…

*"do unto others as you would have them do unto you"! (Luke 6:31)*

One practical way to love others better is to build empathy with them by imagining ourselves in their shoes. The conscious reflection of how we might like to be treated in a particular circumstance gives us a better chance of being able to build rapport with people around us as we make allowances for their individual needs and desires. For instance do we like to be treated with love and respect? Do we feel that it is our right to be heard and understood? Then this is a clear indication of how we should be responding to those around us if we are really serious about building positive healthy relationships.

## 4. The habit of Preferring: treating other people like VIP's

*"Do nothing out of selfish ambition or vain conceit. Rather, in humility value others above yourselves." Philippians 2:3*

In order to maximise our relationships we will first have to get rid of our desire to always be on top, to always be right and to be first in line. There is no room for a selfish competitive spirit in healthy relationships. This goes against cultural norms and the overall direction of our overtly individualistic society.

However if we seriously believe that Jesus is the way to life, then his call to love one another is a call:
– to "esteem others as better than self"
– to "serve one another"
– to "bear one another's burdens"
– to "honour one another"

These principles are so radical that when they are sincerely embraced they can revolutionise communities, marriages and organisations around the globe.

Unfortunately the attitude of many in our world is "I have to win." "I have to prove that I am more important than you." We have all seen the consequences of such attitudes in the violence and strife that pervades our daily experience of life in the 21st century. Therefore if we want to maximise our relationships we must become revolutionaries whose propaganda is love and whose cause is reconciliation. Our attitude must be "I want to help you win." "I want to help you feel valued." After all isn't that how we would want others to treat us?

However what if we make the first move and then discover that we don't get the same treatment in return? Is that a risk worth taking? Will people take advantage of us?

Once again our model is Jesus *"Who, being in very nature God, did not consider equality with God something to be used to his own advantage; rather, he made himself nothing by taking the very nature of a servant, being made in human likeness. And being found in appearance as a man, he humbled himself by becoming obedient to death – even death on a cross!"*

Philippians 2:6-8

## Application:
### reflect on the following questions

- When did you last deliberately put someone else first? How did that feel?

- When did you allow yourself to lose out on something you wanted in order to help someone else get what they wanted or needed? How did that feel?

- When did you last give someone the benefit of the doubt? How did that feel?

Chapter Five

# Four Barriers to maximising potential.

**Principle: Performance = Potential Minus Interference ... or in other words our performance will only ever be as good as our ability to successfully get rid of elements of interference that erode our ability to be effective.**

There are many barriers which reduce our effectiveness in life but the following four areas are perhaps the most obvious and easily recognizable and because of that if we can deal with them we immediately experience improvements in the quality of our lives and our overall performance. We will therefore briefly discuss the following barriers

1. Anxious Fear

2. Disappointment

3. Condemnation

4. Wrong or unhelpful beliefs and values

## Fear/anxiety

"The will to do springs from the knowledge that we can do. Doubt and fear are the great enemies of knowledge, and he who encourages them, who does not slay them, thwarts himself at every step."

*Allen, James. As a Man Thinketh: A Guide to Unlocking the Power of Your Mind.*

**Fear** is a negative emotional state triggered by the presence of a stimulus that has the potential to cause harm, and **Anxiety** is a negative emotional state in which the threat is not present but anticipated. It is worth noting initially that fear can be a good thing in some situations as it helps us cope with life's challenges. But when these states interfere with our ability to survive and thrive, it has become a barrier and a problem that needs dealing with.

So when is fear unhelpful?

When someone says he is afraid of failing a driving test or becoming a victim of crime, he should, by the definitions above, be saying he is anxious instead. So for the purposes of this discussion we will mainly be thinking about anxiety or fear that is imagined and anticipated even when it is not real or present.

Anxiety related fear has the power to hold us back from taking risks, following our dreams, or becoming successful at anything we attempt to do. If we allows it to control us for long enough, it can eventually erode our quality of life, our health and keep us locked in a prison of inactivity. It is a sad fact that fear/anxiety holds more people back than lack of opportunity or talent!

There are many types of anxious fear and these include

- Fear of the future
- Fear of rejection
- Fear of success
- Fear of failure
- Fear of people

The Bible unsurprisingly has a lot to say about fear and is littered with strong encouragements to reject fear and focus on living in God's Love which "casts out fear" and trust in the God who is faithful to all His promises and loving to all He has made (Psalms 145)

According to the Bible *"The fear of man casts a snare "but conversely "the fear (honour respect) of the Lord is the beginning of wisdom"*. Proverbs 29:25 and Proverbs 1:7

## Five 'true-isms' about fear!

1. Most of the things we are afraid about never actually come to pass

2. Most anxious fears are imagined rather than real

3. Many fears are irrational and based on lies that we have believed or been told

4. Rational fears such as fear of being burned by fire are good fears designed to protect us

5. Fear is False Evidence Appearing Real!

## Disappointment

Disappointment is the experience of sadness involving unfulfiled hopes or expectations and it comes upon us with a heavy sense of recognition that we don't have, didn't get, or will never achieve whatever it is that we wanted. These expectations may have been too high, irrational or unrealistic but the resulting feeling of being "let down" can be debilitating. Psychologists agree that continuous exposure to unmet expectations and a lack of coping strategies seriously threatens the emotional and physical well being of a person, resulting in symptoms and effects such as depression, anger, apathy, denial and fear.

Disappointments come from a variety of sources...

**Life can let us down:** even the best laid plans can come to nothing and the best of intentions can end up crushed in the dust of dashed dreams and there are times when we may be tempted to ask "why do I bother"? There are some things in life that we just can't control and therefore pinning our hopes and dreams upon an ideal set of circumstances makes us vulnerable to the impact of the unknown and the unexpected.

**Friends and family let us down:** The people that we love and put our trust in are the ones with the most power to let us down and when they do the pain is sharp and goes deep. Trusting people becomes difficult when we have been badly let down by them and the bitterness that results from broken promises and the betrayal of confidences can often spell the end of that friendship unless the parties are prepared to work hard on forgiving and making restitution.

**We can let ourselves down:** not living up to our own expectations is a common experience which is often caused by having expectations which are unrealistic or just misplaced. Surprisingly it is not necessarily because our expectations are too high but according to Michelangelo's ancient observation about humanity, the converse is often true:

*"It's not that we aim too high and we miss it but that we aim to low and hit it".*

Either way the result is the same we end up with regret and feel frustrated with ourselves and our inner critic asks us "Have you really got what it takes"?

**We can feel let down by God:**

Where is God when it hurts? Why does God seem silent and distant?

The results of experiencing disappointment can leave us stuck in a very unhelpful place where we are afraid to believe for good things in our future and therefore choose not to set goals, take risks or have any sense of expectation for the future. If this state continues for a long time then we can very easily become filled with self pity, ending up being negative and cynical about our lives and our destiny, which is the exact opposite of how God wants us to be. After all He is revealed in the scriptures as the God of all hope and our loving heavenly father who delights to give good gifts to his children and in whom there is no trace of inconsistency.

The Psalms recount in often explicit detail the effects and reality of opposition, disappointment and betrayal that life often throws at us. Equally they also celebrate the powerful impact of trusting in the promises and faithfulness of the living God. In Psalm 27 the psalmist makes a great declaration that contains within it the antidote to all disappointment…<u>Biblical Hope!</u>

*"What would have become of me if I had not believed that I would see the goodness of the Lord in the land of the living"! Psalm 27:21*

Biblical hope or the confident expectation of good things from the hand of God is a powerful life enhancing force and significantly undermines the power of disappointment to cripple us and prevent us from moving forward in an effective manner.

This kind of hope or the cultivating of a positive imagination helps to build a sense of confidence for the future and a belief that whatever happens, God is for us and if He is for us then who or what can ever stand against us and win? This is a hope that will never disappoint us based at it is on the character of God, His principles and His promises all of which are completely and unwaveringly faithful and true.

## Wrong beliefs and values

Our values are near the core of our identity. They are the things we judge to be good for us and others. Some values and beliefs are helpful whilst some are very unhelpful.

A simple but helpful definition of a value is: "something (as a principle or quality) intrinsically valuable or desirable." At one level, values are the ideals, customs, and institutions of a society.

When judged by a biblical standard, these values may be positive (education, freedom), neutral (cleanliness), or negative (cruelty, crime, blasphemy). We can also think of values as objects or qualities that are desirable as ends in themselves.

Every person holds a unique set of values but the main question is …

*Are your values and beliefs helping you or hindering you?*

At school I remember being told by teachers that I "could do better" so for many years I always had a feeling that anything I did was never quite good enough and could always be done better by someone else. This belief was also compounded by something my mother jokingly called me which may have contained some truth, but did not help my self-image or improve my prospects. She called me on some occasions "half-finished Eric" because I was as a youngster not a good finisher. These statements impacted me is a subtle way that caused me to feel that my work was somehow inferior and therefore I never expected to excel at anything. This became an underlying belief which I think stopped me reaching higher than I could have done in some respects, certainly in my early twenties. I was disempowered because I always had the sense that I was just "average".

This was a belief that did not help me and it was not until God began to show me that far from being "average" I was in fact "unique" that I began to change that belief and renewed my thinking in this area. Something that also helped in this regard was discovering and understanding my personality preferences (using various psychometric tests such as Belbin's team roles and Myers Briggs) that I was actually someone who enjoyed and excelled at starting projects but that I was not a natural completer finisher. So my mother had observed in me something that was true but had perhaps understandably interpreted it as a negative. Through greater understanding and access to better information I now can see that the flip side of my weakness contains tremendous strength. This also makes me realise how much I need other people around me to make up for the downsides of my personality preferences and helps me appreciate the vital importance of team working.

**Application:** Let's pause for a moment to ask a few questions about the values we hold to try and understand if this is an area where we are experiencing the negative effects of wrong values and beliefs.

*Where did you get your values and beliefs from?*

*Do your values and beliefs match up with a biblical world view and or the values of Jesus?*

*Have you thought of renewing your thinking about something so that you deliberately change a negative value into a positive helpful one?*

## Chapter Six

# Five keys to get us over the barriers

### Principle: We can do all things through Christ who strengthens us!

Having acknowledged and identified that there are some barriers that we will need to overcome in order to become what we were made to be, it is important that we don't focus on them. It has been said that what we focus on is what we end up getting and so by focusing on the strengths and abilities that we do have and drawing upon Gods wisdom and strength which is available to us in the power of the Holy Spirit we can become more than conquerors and over comers rather than victims and failures.

In fact it's really important to recalibrate our understanding of failure and appreciate that: Failure is an event, not a person. In addition any person who has been successful will tell you that success in any field only comes after some failure has been experienced in the first place.

Failure in essence is really just constructive feedback that tells us how not to do something so that we can change our approach in order to get better results.

*"There is no failure...only feedback."* — *Robert Allen*

*"Failure is an event, never a person."* — *William D. Brown*

With that in mind let's look at four keys that will help us in practical ways to overcome the barriers described in the previous chapter and work towards maximising our potential.

- Key 1: Possibility thinking or developing a positive mindset.

- Key 2: Purposeful living or being intentional.

- Key 3: Proactive effort... taking responsibility

- Key 4: Passion for God... loving God by doing His will.

- Key 5: Persistence... keeping on keeping on

## Key 1: Possibility thinking or developing a positive imagination.

*"If you think you can you can, but if you think you can't you are probably right"* Henry Ford

The idea of a positive mental attitude has been around for a long time but more and more evidence is coming to light through the field of Positive Psychology that has uncovered many benefits to cultivating positive thinking or an optimistic attitude to life.

## Positive Thinkers Cope Better With Stress

When faced with stressful situations, positive thinkers cope more effectively than pessimists. In one study, researchers found that when optimists encounter a disappointment (such as not getting a job or promotion) they are more likely to focus on things they can do to resolve the situation. Rather than dwelling on their frustrations or things that they cannot change, they will devise a plan of action and ask others for assistance and advice. Pessimists, on the other hand, simply assume that the situation is out of their control and there is nothing they can do to change it.

## Optimism Can Improve Your Immunity

In recent years, researchers have found that your mind can have a powerful effect on your body. Immunity is one area where your thoughts and attitudes can have a particularly powerful influence. In one study, researchers found that activation in brain areas associated with negative emotions led to a weaker immune response to a flu vaccine.

## Positive Thinking Is Good for Your Health

Not only can positive thinking impact your ability to cope with stress and your immunity, it also has an impact on your overall well-being. Some health professionals have reported a number of health benefits associated with optimism, including a reduced risk of death from cardiovascular problems, less depression, and an increased lifespan.

## It Can Make You More Resilient

Resilient people are able to face a crisis or trauma with strength and resolve, rather than falling apart. It may come as no surprise to learn that positive thinking can play a major role in resilience. When dealing with a challenge, optimists typically look at what they can do to fix the problem. Instead of giving up hope, they marshal their resources and are willing to ask others for help.

**But wait a minute!** – This information should not really be news for those of us who have some working knowledge of the Bible because much of the above research simply confirms what various biblical writers were saying thousands of years ago.

Paul, the writer of much of the New Testament, encouraged his readers to *"Fix your thoughts on what is true and good and right"* (Phil 4:8 TLB). And called on them to *"Renew their thinking so that they could know what was good, perfect and acceptable"* (2 Corinthians 12:1,2).

The writer of Proverbs pointed out that *"A cheerful heart is good medicine, but a crushed spirit dries up the bones and famously declared that "As a man thinks so he is!"* (Proverbs 23:7)

In the book By I H Allen "As a Man thinks" the author makes the following observations

*"Every action and feeling is preceded by a thought."* And *"A man is literally what he thinks, his character being the complete sum of all his thoughts."*

So from the scientific evidence as well as biblical and other philosophical writings it seems proven that our thinking is central to the outcomes of our lives. The thoughts we cultivate drive how we feel which in the end often drive how we behave.

If you stop to think about this you already know how this works in the negative. We are all very good at using our imaginations to create worst case scenarios that keep us awake all night as the images and thoughts create fear and dread which always seems worse in the midnight hours.

How vital and practical then that we can begin to choose to use our thoughts to harness the energy of a positive imagination, to see ourselves as God sees us and to focus on what He has said about us and the good things He has promised for us.

It seems then that Christians should really be the prime examples of positive thinking. When we consider how much God is for us and how often in the scriptures He has promised to be with us.

*"For I know the plans I have for you says the Lord, plans to prosper you not to harm you, plans to give you hope and a future" Jeremiah 29:11 NIV*

*"You will keep him in perfect peace, whose mind is stayed on you, because he trusts in you." Isaiah 26:3 NKJV*

## Key 2: Purposeful living or being intentional.

A life of significance requires planning and preparation, It will not happen by accident or by chance. If we want to make a change we may need to become the change, if we want to make a difference we will need to behave differently. If we want to have impact we will first of all need to allow ourselves to be impacted. All this requires intentionality and a commitment to living like we really mean it!

According to Dr Randy Carlson of The Intentional Living Centre (www.theintentionallife.com) there are five areas where we can start planning to be more intentional, which will have far reaching implications in our ability to overcome barriers and reach towards our potential.

- ✓ Faith: the key to knowing and pleasing God. Are we planning to walk the talk!

- ✓ Family: Family is God's idea and an essential area of our lives. If our family hurts, we hurt. Building families is an intentional process

- ✓ Finances: managing money is a must for anybody serious about being a maximiser.

- ✓ Health: looking after our body makes sense. It's the only one we've got and without it there is not much we can achieve at all. When was the last time you had a medical check-up? Do you take exercise regularly?

- ✓ Work/career: maintaining a work life balance is an ongoing challenge for all of us but like money our work needs to be managed in order for it to remain enjoyable and productive. So are you working to live or living to work?

Dr Carlson argues that if we are really serious about following Jesus then we need to find out what pleases him in every context of our lives and start doing it!

## Key 3: Proactive effort...taking responsibility.

The Apostle Peter was a great example of a proactive person and in 2 Peter 1:3-8 he lists seven habits that he says will produce a greater and ever increasing level of fruitfulness in our lives as we intentionally make the effort to continually add them to our lifestyle.

*³Gods divine power has given us everything we need for life and godliness through our knowledge of him who called us by his own glory and goodness. ⁴Through these he has given us his very great and precious promises, so that through them we may participate in the divine nature and escape the corruption in the world caused by evil desires.*

*[5]For this very reason, make every effort to add to your faith goodness; and to goodness, knowledge; [6]and to knowledge, self-control; and to self-control, perseverance; and to perseverance, godliness; [7]and to godliness, brotherly kindness; and to brotherly kindness, love. [8]For if we possess these qualities in increasing measure; they will keep us from being ineffective and unproductive in our knowledge of our Lord Jesus Christ.*

**To summarise, Peter seems to be outlining the seven habits of a successful Christian!**

- Goodness: moral excellence: continuous improvement

- Knowledge: understanding/insight

- Self control: discipline/consistency

- Perseverance: courage, commitment and determination

- Godliness: Spiritual Perspectives and priorities

- Brotherly Kindness: it's not just about me/community/family

- Love: unconditional love…the highest aspiration.

If this is how Peter encourages the early church to live in order for them to be fruitful and effective in their lives on earth let's take a few lessons from the man who got out of the boat and walked on water, preached up a storm on the day of Pentecost and whose declaration of faith was the rock on which Christ built his church. He walked the talk and so can we!

It all starts with the fact that God has already taken the initiative and has already done everything that needs to be done to provide a way for us to be saved from our selfishness and be restored to the family of God with all the privileges and responsibilities that entails.

God has made his move; He has given us His power and His promises which leaves the ball very firmly in our court. What is our response going to be?

After an initial response of faith which is the process where we reach out and receive what God has already given, our ongoing response to God's provision subsequently is to intentionally and pro-actively practice **making every effort** to add to that faith, habits that will stop us from becoming lazy and unproductive in our faith and will by implication cause us to be effective, productive, fruitful and successful followers of Jesus.

*(See chapter 7 for a fuller discussion on these 7 factors)*

## Key 4: Passion for God.... loving God by doing His will.

We are made for God's pleasure so it makes sense that as we seek to please God we naturally maximise our lives wherever we are on the journey. Ephesians 5:10 (The Message) says *"Figure out what will please Christ and then do it."* This is the heart of true worship, a lifestyle of pleasing God by doing the right thing, serving our neighbour and loving God with our whole being and not just on Sunday. Like most things this passion begins in the mind first and foremost before it effects the emotions:

*"For the soul of a person to be inflamed with passion for the living God, that person's mind must first be informed about the character and will of God. There can be nothing in the heart that is not first in the mind. Though it is possible to have theology on the head without its piercing the soul, it cannot pierce the soul without first being grasped by the mind"*. R.C. Sproul

## Key 5 Persistence Perseverance:

We have already discussed this habit in chapter 2 and will be talking about it again in chapter 7 so for now let's just end with a poem by an unknown author which superbly captures the essence of the perseverance principle:

## DON'T QUIT!!

When things go wrong, as they sometimes will,
When the road you're trudging seems all uphill,
When the funds are low and the debts are high,
And you want to smile, but you have to sigh,
When care is pressing you down a bit,
Rest, if you must, but don't you quit.

Life is queer with its twists and turns,
As every one of us sometimes learns,
And many a failure turns about,
When he might have won had he stuck it out;
Don't give up though the pace seems slow—
You may succeed with another blow.

Often the goal is nearer than,
It seems to a faint and faltering man,
Often the struggler has given up,
When he might have captured the victor's cup,
And he learned too late when the night slipped down,
How close he was to the golden crown.

Success is failure turned inside out—
The silver tint of the clouds of doubt,
And you never can tell how close you are,
It may be near when it seems so far,
So stick to the fight when you're hardest hit—
It's when things seem worst that you must not quit.

## Chapter Seven

# Making every effort...

**Principle: Making an effort is the foundational key to becoming a maximiser.**

*"As human beings, we are responsible for our own lives. Our behaviour is a function of our decisions, not our conditions. We can subordinate feelings to values." Steven Covey*

Victor Frankl, in his phenomenal work, "Man's Search for Meaning", talks extensively about being proactive. As he lived through the horror of the Nazi concentration camps, Frankl noticed that there was a distinct difference between those who were able to survive (and sometimes even thrive) during that experience and those who gave up. This was in essence the ability to be proactive in deciding how they were going to respond to that ordeal. The Nazis may have been able to take away their liberty, but the freedom of how they would choose to respond would always remain with them.

This proactive habit principle is borne out in many biblical writings:

*"Love one another" Jesus. Love here is a doing word requiring proactive effort.*

*Ecclesiastes:9:10 "Whatsoever your hand finds to do, do it with all your might."*

*Proverbs 4:23 "..above everything else guard your heart for everything you do flows from it."*

In the last chapter we touched on 2 Peter 1:3-(9)8 where Peter is urging his readers to "make every effort" in adding seven particular habits to their faith. Let's look a little bit closer at each of these seven habits because according to Peter the addition of these factors into our lives will guarantee fruitfulness and effectiveness and surely those are the key components of maximising our potential.

## Lets start by re reading the passage:

*[3]Gods divine power has given us everything we need for life and godliness through our knowledge of him who called us by his own glory and goodness.[4]Through these he has given us his very great and precious promises, so that through them we may participate in the divine nature and escape the corruption in the world caused by evil desires.*

*[5]For this very reason, make every effort to add to your faith goodness; and to goodness, knowledge; [6]and to knowledge, self-control; and to self-control, perseverance; and to perseverance, godliness; [7]and to godliness, brotherly kindness; and to brotherly kindness, love. [8]For if we possess these*

*qualities in increasing measure; they will keep us from being ineffective and unproductive in our knowledge of our Lord Jesus Christ.*

Notice that the first five habits are all focused on our responsibility to take care of what's going on in our personal lives within the context of our relationship with God, whilst the last two habits are to do with how we are interacting with others around us in both the Church and in the wider world.

This is very similar to the principles described by Steven Covey in his book Seven habits of Effective People and although the habits listed in our biblical passage are not the same there are many similarities and cross over's.

Covey referred to it like this: *"Every public victory is preceded by a private victory..."and regarding proactive habits that"The proactive approach is to change from the 'inside-out': to be different, and by being different, to effect positive change in what's out there – I can be more resourceful, I can be more diligent, I can be more creative, I can be more cooperative."*

Let's see what Peter's seven biblical based habits have to teach us.

# Goodness/virtue/Moral Excellence

**Practical right living according to Gods standard or "doing the right thing"!**

Moral Excellence is a trait of the Divine Nature rather than the Human Nature. It does not come naturally to us. It must be sought for, cultivated, and developed. In fact we already know that without God's help we will ultimately fall short of His standards. That's why we need to start from a place of faith, being found "in Christ…not having a righteousness of our own but that which is by faith"

In Classical times virtue meant 'that quality given by the gods which enabled mere mortal men to perform heroic deeds.' It came to mean the quality in a person's life which made them stand-out as excellent. It is a term of moral heroism, moral courage, moral excellence. We understand that morality is the defining of what is right and wrong. Virtue then is the courageous and heroic decision to always do what is right. It is both to keep one's self pure from wickedness and depravity AND to perform acts of righteousness. As soon as morality is mentioned, there are those who object on the grounds that each person's opinion is his or her own and equal to that of anyone else. In our post modern world everything is considered relative including truth and so for those who think like that there can be no objective and commonly agreed upon moral norm. For such persons, morality is an illusion. However for those who have trusted in Christ it is a higher calling which requires us to intentionally live up to who we are in Him.

*"faith without works (i.e. moral excellence) is dead!" James 2:17*

## Reflective questions

- Do you have any habits or standards of behaviour which you know do not conform to God's standards?

- How long will you allow them to stop you maximising your potential?

- Do you believe that God's power and promises really do help you escape corruption caused by evil desires or do you feel powerless to live up to God's expectations?

- What do you intend to do about it?

## Knowledge

There are many kinds of knowledge that we could add to our faith and it is fair to say that acquiring knowledge is a great and very positive habit to adopt in the pursuit of lifelong learning. However in this particular context there is an implicit suggestion that Peter is talking primarily about the knowledge of God, his character and his ways.

Knowing God is described by Jesus as the very essence of what is meant by the phrase "eternal life", this kind of life is not just about longevity but about a superior quality of life that is often described as "life in all its fullness"!

- Knowing God's Will: what God wants us to do.

- Knowing God's Word: what God has said about pretty much everything!

- Knowing God's Works: seeing God at work in us and through us.

- Knowing God's Ways: understanding Gods Character and motivation

## Practicing the habit of adding Knowledge?

- Through the disciplines of reading the scriptures which are described as the word of God,

- Spending time with God in prayer and meditation enjoying His presence,

- Fellowshipping with Gods people as they worship together and live lives committed to pleasing Him.

- Listening to practical teaching at your local church, at conferences and workshops and via the many online podcasts and video presentations which abound on the internet.

- Reading books that help us to increase our

knowledge and understanding of who God is and how He is working in our world today.

- Find a spiritual mentor who can help and inspire us in our relationship with God.

Make notes every time you read a book or listen to a sermon in order to underline the learning points you are receiving in the moment and then create a filing system so you can retrieve the information later. (www.evernote.com will help with this)

## Self control:

There is a difference between knowing what and how to do the right thing and the actual doing of the right thing and that difference is in the area of self control. Like many worthwhile habits self control requires effort and practice and a level of internal motivation which is firmly grounded in the values and beliefs embodied in the previous two habits of Goodness and Knowledge.

### Practical application questions.

- What area do you struggle to control in your life?
- What positive difference would it make If you could get control back?
- What is stopping you from making that happen?
- What would the effect of simply giving up be?
- What is the alternative?

## Perseverance

Author and speaker Michael Hyatt says *"The truth is that we learn the best lessons when we don't quit. This is when our character is transformed and good things happen"*.

Perseverance is the choice we need to make to keep on keeping on when the going gets tough. It's a choice or decision that only we can make and the making of that choice can be the difference between success and failure. It is a truism that anything that is really worth doing is going to require a level of commitment above and beyond the ordinary in order to be successful and there is no way around that reality. The reward of perseverance is that we prove ourselves, our faith and the faithfulness of the one who calls us to make the choice. The result is that we become people of confident expectation who believe that they can win and have decided to keep going, to keep the faith, so that we can reach the goal and win the prize.

### Practical application

- Where and when are you tempted to give up?
- Why are you going to keep going?
- What is at stake if you do quit?

*Make a list of positive reasons for keeping going towards your goals and for maintaining faith and integrity in your life. Keep adding to your list as various challenges tempt you think about giving up. Remember always ask yourself Why and how should I keep going? Rather than why shouldn't I quit?*

## Godliness

The habit of making God our first point of reference, our number one priority , our anchor in the storms of life, the focus of our energy and the source of our motivation, the foundation we build upon and the example we aspire to. This is the essence of being a living sacrifice, a bond slave of Christ, being sold out for Jesus, a Jesus freak , a fool for Jesus.

I like the way King Solomon says it: *"Trust in the Lord with all your heart and don't lean on your own understanding, in all your ways acknowledge him and he will direct your paths". Proverbs 3:24*

Major Ian Thomas said it another way…*"True godliness leaves the world convinced beyond a shadow of a doubt, that the only explanation for you, is Jesus Christ to whose eternally unchanging and altogether adequate "I AM!" your heart has learned to say with unshatterable faith, "Thou art!"*

I have always thought that my father was a "godly man" and aspire to be like him in many ways. He was by no means perfect; however there was strength of Godly character and solidity of faith that consistently shone through in his daily life. This was never truer than when at the age of 58 he lay dying of cancer after a brief period of illness. On the day he was told that he had five weeks to live he said in response to my suggestion of praying for him,

*"You can certainly pray for me but when you do make it mostly praise".*

At the time I found that very challenging, because I wanted to pray for healing above everything else and the last thing I felt like doing was praising. However my father had a different focus and as he looked death in the face, his heart was fixed securely on the perfect healing and rest that comes in God's presence for eternity. Years later the implication of that faith-filled, challenging response resonates inside me as I recognise how strongly his life was founded on his relationship with God and the absolute certainty in the midst of the ultimate test of faith that God was his anchor not just in this life but for eternity.

Over twenty years later I heard from a friend who had visited my father in those final weeks and after spending two hours talking and praying together he recounted that, although he had gone to comfort my father, in the end the strength of faith and resolve he had found in his company had profoundly encouraged and challenged him in his own walk with God. I know many others found the same to be true.

### How can we practice Godliness?

- Acknowledging God in all our ways
- Involving God in all our plans
- Carrying on a conversation with God throughout the day which was described by Brother Lawrence as "Practicing the Presence of God".

## Brotherly kindness: how we interact with our brothers and sisters "in Christ".

When I was 18 years old I joined the police force and went off to the training school for a 10 week course of training before being posted to my duty station. During this time I had several eye opening moments as this was the first time away from home and living in close proximity to a bunch of guys who were friendly enough but in no way had any particular reverence for the things of God. I was known as Christian and they respected or perhaps tolerated my faith but that was as far as it went.

However, on one weekend I was required to stay in the training school instead of going home and on Sunday I decided to try and find a church to attend. I found a bus stop opposite the police college and waited armed only with a street name where I had learned there was a church of the same denomination that I was used to attending. A few minutes later a car pulled up at the bus stop and the driver informed me that no buses were running that day and asked if he could give me a lift into town. After telling him the name of the church I wanted to go to he said that he knew the place and would drop me off outside. I was very thankful and aware of God's provision in such a practical way, but that was just the beginning!

Once inside the church I will always remember the very warm welcome I was given and at the end of the service I was immediately invited out to lunch with one of the families. After a lovely roast dinner they enthusiastically persuaded me to stay on for tea and attend the youth event that was being held in their home that evening. I gladly accepted and had a fantastic time of fellowship, some lovely food and even got a lift back to the training school at the end of the day.

When I walked back into the block where I was living some of the other men were quite concerned as to where I had been all day and were worried that something untoward had happened to me.

"Where on earth have you been all day, we thought you'd got lost or something"?

So I told them how my day had been and to my surprise they were genuinely shocked by my story and began to ask questions.

"What! Someone you had never met before invited

you for a Sunday Roast and then gave you tea as well?! Are you sure you didn't know these people?" They were incredulous and I think, a little grudgingly, impressed.

I myself was very grateful but not surprised by these events because growing up in a Christian home I had many times seen my parents providing generous hospitality to strangers and visiting Christians at my home church. To me it was really the norm and part of being in the body of Christ. What stood out for me that day was the shocked reaction from my non Christian friends that I could have spent a full day being entertained and so well looked after by people who, until that morning, were complete strangers.

This simple display of "brotherly kindness" was possibly the most powerful testimony that my colleagues had ever heard and clearly demonstrated the words of Jesus when he said

*"Love one another (brotherly kindness) for by this shall all men know that you are disciples."*

How we treat each other speaks volumes about the level and genuine nature of our faith. It's a habit we are encouraged to cultivate and in doing so we will be a blessing and receive many blessings in return.

Jesus said *"Freely you have received, therefore freely give!"*

### How can we practice brotherly kindness?

- When was the last time you invited someone out for lunch or dinner?
- When did you last serve someone without being asked?
- Are you regularly performing random acts of kindness?
- What needs to change in order for those Random acts to become more intentional?

## Love: the ultimate goal

Each of these habits or qualities discussed so far are described as being produced in the context of the preceding quality: each habit seems to grow out of the soil and climate of the other. In addition, the new quality supplements and perfects the preceding one until we reach the ultimate habit which is love. Love being the very nature of God is the goal which is the epitome of Christ-like service and lifestyle as described so beautifully in 1 Corinthians 13.

*"If I speak in the tongues of mortals and of angels, but do not have love, I am a noisy gong or a clanging cymbal. And if I have prophetic powers, and understand all mysteries and all knowledge, and if I have all faith, so as to remove mountains, but do not have love, I am nothing. If I give away all*

*my possessions, and if I hand over my body so that I may boast, but do not have love, I gain nothing. Love is patient; love is kind; love is not envious or boastful or arrogant or rude. It does not insist on its own way; it is not irritable or resentful; it does not rejoice in wrongdoing, but rejoices in the truth. It bears all things, believes all things, hopes all things, endures all things. Love never ends"*

Love is a doing word and therefore is grounded in everyday living and not in some mystical experience. To live like this must surely be to maximise our true potential and to become everything that we were made to be.

*God is love and those who live in Him, live in Love 1 John 1:12*

However the point that Peter seems to be making in 2 Peter 2:3-9 is that we cannot practice the love habit effectively without first growing in the other habits described beforehand. This is not to say that we cannot produce love until we have produced all these qualities to maturity, but that there is a progression and a mutual dependency, in that we can show love only to the degree that we are developing the other qualities.

In other words each quality becomes the productive sphere or the soil out of which the next quality flourishes and becomes mature, eventually achieving a functional and eminently practical spiritual synergy that is the embodiment of the Apostle Paul's statement

> *"The only thing that counts is faith working itself out through love"*
>
> *Galations 5:6*

## Reflective questions

- Can you identify parts of your life where you are intentionally adding love to your faith?
- What type of effort/action is required to maximise this habit in your life?

Chapter Eight

# Discovering life purpose and calling

### Principle: You are made for something?

So far we have discovered that Success is intentionally making the effort to maximise our own unique potential in each and every situation, regardless of whether the circumstances are helping us or hindering us. In this context we have discussed that:

### Maximising our potential is becoming everything that we were made to be.

*We have outlined that this begins by getting to know the God who made us and living in relationship with Him. Having found peace with God through faith we then take responsibility to make every effort to add value to that faith by increasing and improve our resources, our reality and our relationships by using five keys of:*

- Possibility thinking or developing a positive mindset.

- Purposeful living or being intentional.

- Proactive effort... taking responsibility

- Passion for God... loving God by doing His will.

- Persistence… keeping on keeping on

Whilst at the same time resisting fear disappointment and guilt…

Ultimately however it is very hard to become everything that we were made to be if we don't know what we were made for in the first place. It is not possible to truly fulfil our life's purpose until we first (of all) find out what it is.

**Discovering our core purpose is therefore essential to truly maximising potential and to being able to live life with intention or, in other words, to live everyday like we really mean it!**

As a coach I love asking questions, I am curious and sincerely interested in the answers to powerful and meaningful questions about life and purpose and destiny and I believe this passion began with someone asking me one such question.

It was just after my thirtieth birthday and I was in a period of wondering about where my life was going and what I should be doing with it. I had been married for three years and had two very young children and at that time was working for my father in the family business. Previously I had been involved for three years with Youth with a Mission working in Liverpool UK delivering faith based programs for young people across the Merseyside area, and before that had spent almost six years as a police officer in Cumbria. So I had been involved in a wide variety of jobs and ministries none of which seemed to have any real common thread and it certainly was not a career path to get too excited about. However, I felt that I had sincerely been seeking to follow God's leading as far as I was aware of it and believed, even in my restlessness, that somehow there was a plan to all this. But I couldn't see any overall purpose or a path down which I could walk with intention and vision.

One evening we had friends over for dinner and as we chatted afterwards over a coffee my friend asked me something which immediately caused my heart to leap in anticipation that something significant was being communicated. His question was simply this…

**'Have you ever asked God…"What am I made for"?'**

Wow! What a question! I can't remember what answer I specifically gave, but as I pondered that question I quickly realised that despite many years of being a committed Christian I had never really asked that question is such a direct way in any of my conversations with God. I believed that there was a plan and a purpose but could not put a name to it or explain in detail what it was. I also realised that this question was the very articulation of all the other questions that I had been asking myself over the previous months as I pondered my life but had never had the courage to address that question to the only One who could provide me with an answer. I think, if I am honest, there was a belief or maybe a fear that God would never answer such a direct question and perhaps I thought that He would rather keep me guessing than give me a direct answer. Therefore to hear someone else even suggesting that it was a valid question to ask was liberating and exciting. My immediate desire was to know how one went about asking or preparing to hear an answer to such a profound question. After a brief discussion this is what I ended up doing.

I planned to spend a full day away from all distractions when I could focus on thinking and praying about my life purpose and literally ask God "what am I made for?" I ended up using the front room of a friend who was away for the weekend and I spent the time talking to God and listening in the silence for his replies, worshipping Him, reading the scriptures, re-reading old notes that I had made over the years to try and discover themes and trends in how God had led me so far and to remind myself of the words and scriptures which had been influential in giving me direction up to that point. I asked myself what I had enjoyed doing and what I had been successful in; what feedback had other people whom I respected given to me about my gifts and talents. I expected a flash of lightning inspiration and some kind of mystical experience but instead there was a growing realization and a strong affirmation of so many things that I already knew but I had not taken the time to join all the dots before.

At the end of the day I came away with a phrase that, for me, summed up what I was convinced God has shown me through the course of the time spent seeking Him – and that phrase was just two words: **Developing People!** I had no more details and no specifics, but this statement gave me a framework to focus on and a sense of purpose which I could now begin to work out with some real intention, confident that this was the area where God wanted me to focus my energies and gifting. I was excited and couldn't wait to get on with whatever "developing people" was all about. I also realised that in some respects I had already been working out this purpose in various ways which, up to that point perhaps, seemed to be a random series of circumstances. But now there was something to aim for and a framework in which to get intentional.

At the time I interpreted the call to develop people as being only within the context of Church and as I was in a position of leadership at the time in a small local fellowship I could easily see how this vision could be worked out, which was encouraging. However as my life developed and changed I found myself realizing that this call was much broader and I began to understand that it was to be fulfiled not only within the church context but also in the personal development industry and the business world. I can now see how God was drawing all the various experiences of my life together so that I could make a greater impact than I had previously thought possible.

As a result of focusing on developing people as a life purpose I have ended up studying for a teaching qualification, training to be a life coach, training leaders in small and large companies, travelling to other nations and taking up a job as a business advisor. All of those events and opportunities came about as I began to pro-actively focus on doing what I believed I was "made for" in each and every situation in which I found myself. I did what I could to make things happen and trusted God to do what I could not do and to enable and equip me with the resources to make it all work.

## Practical exercise:
## Write your personal mission statement.

Write a personal life mission statement using the reflective questions below. Begin by answering the questions as fully and as honestly as you can. Secondly, using your answers, construct a short sentence or series of statements that summarise what your life is all about. **Keep reviewing and developing it** over time to reflect new insights and new experiences.

My own mission statement started out as:

*"Helping people to maximise their unique potential".*

...that was in 2003.

In 2010 it was:

*"I help people become everything that they were made to be". I kept reviewing and developing the central ideas behind it"*

...and now, in 2014, it reads:

*"I help people to discover their unique identity so that they can live with integrity, increase their influence and make a significant impact."*

## How do you begin to explore your life's purpose from a Biblical perspective?

The following questions, given time and an honest response, will get you thinking along the right lines. Grab some paper right now and record your thoughts and ideas and see what begins to emerge.

◊ What desires and deeply felt dreams have you been aware of in your life?

◊ What is it that motivates you to be productive?

◊ What keeps you going forward when you are weary?

◊ What do you do that gets a positive response from others?

◊ What do other people say you are good at?

- ◊ What activities and or circumstances make you feel fulfiled?

- ◊ What would you still do even if nobody was paying you to do it?

- ◊ What events/periods/seasons in your life have been most enjoyable and have enabled you to make a significant contribution to the outcomes of those events?

- ◊ What have you learned that you could pass on to others by going through difficult and painful life experiences?

- ◊ What need do you feel called and equipped to meet?

- ◊ What people group do you feel called to serve?

- ◊ What areas of life/society are you equipped to add value to?

- ◊ If you had a life message what would it be?

- ◊ Who do you want to serve or make a positive difference with?

- ◊ What scriptures have been influential in your life so far?

- ◊ If you could do, be or have anything at all what would you choose?

So....

Have you ever asked God what you were made for?

What did He say?

---

### Bibliography and recommended reading

The following books have been helpful and inspiring in my own life and have heavily influenced and informed the thinking and conclusions found in this book

- S.H.A.P.E: *Eric Rees*
- Leadership Coaching: *Tony Stolzfus*
- 7 habits of Effective People: *Steven Covey*
- The Purpose Driven Life: *Rick Warren*
- Ordering Your Private World: *George McDonald*
- Mans search for Meaning: *Victor Frankl*
- 15 laws of Growth: *John Maxwell*
- His Image My Image: *Josh McDowell*
- Who do you think you are: *Mark Driscoll*

# About the Author

Eric Barker is a life and business coach combining a wealth of work experience in both the public and private sectors, along with a passion for helping people to maximise their unique potential in life and business. His mission is to encourage people to live with intention and on purpose in order that they can, live with integrity, increase their influence and maximise their impact.

Photo by Martin Sekasi

His greatest joy is enjoying and supporting his wife Joanna and their three daughters. When time allows other interests include playing and listening to music, kayaking in the English Lake District and mountain bike riding.

Eric values integrity and humility, particularly in leadership. His own life choices and personal goals are informed by a passionate commitment to the Christian faith and lifestyle. This commitment has led to an active involvement in local church ministry for over 30 years and he has developed a breadth of experience in teaching /preaching, leading worship, and leadership. In his early twenties he spent three formative years with Youth with a Mission where he gained valuable experience working cross culturally in the UK, Africa and Europe. More recently in 2011/12 he was part of a ministry team delivering discipleship training to Anglican church leaders in Burundi (East Africa).

He is currently studying for a degree in Theology as part of The Anglican Lay Readers training programme within the Diocese of Carlisle, Cumbria.

> For more information, to book a coaching session, or to enquire about having Eric speak at your event you can contact him via the following:
> - Website: www.intentionalheart.co.uk
> - Email: enb159@gmail.com
> - Follow on Twitter: @enb159
> - Facebook page: www.facebook.com/ericbarker
> - Blog: www.ericbarker.blogspot.com